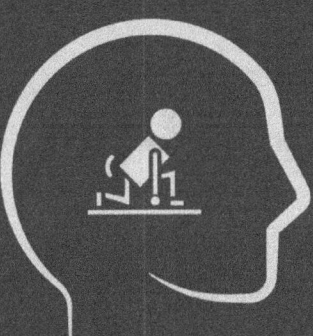

START

Despite The Fear

By Jadesola Onaolapo

START

Despite The Fear

BY

JADESOLA ONAOLAPO

Jadesola Onaolapo
Lekki,
Lagos, Nigeria. 241111
www.jadesolaonaolapo.com

ACKNOWLEDGEMENTS

I have often wondered what my life would be like, if I had not been born when, where and into the family that I have today.

Each time I have those thoughts, I say a huge thanks to God.

For the fact that I'm here in this world, under what I refer to as the imperfect perfect circumstances, I acknowledge your Love and Grace, and I am forever thankful.

I appreciate my family; Dad, Yinkus, Òjògbón Diekola, Dókítà Mofolashade, my darling Afolabi, for your love and support, for always being here, even while I am STILL clearly trying to be at one with myself.

My second Mama and Papa Dr & Mrs Olaoye, I love you.

Dolapo, Tunde and Tejumola (FPNG) Olaoye, I don't have the right words to express my appreciation of you guys. I wonder how I got so lucky to have the best cousins in the entire world.

To my darling lil sis, Jensey Bari, imagine what life would be right now if we never met. I love you beyond words and I'm grateful for your light.

To my best friend Bode Agbe-Davies, I love you and I'm thankful for your kindness, love and unending support. Ride or die, forever.

To my mentor and friend, Victor Ekpo Bassey, you never let me sit in the dark for too long, you made sure to reintroduce me to myself and I'll forever be grateful for that. For all the icecream to wipe away the tears and the stern words to reset my psyche, I'm grateful, more for the icecream sha. Lol.

And lastly, Ms Edirin Edewor, you're a gift that this world needs. I'm super thankful for your encouragement, guidance and support through this process. May you continue to grow in love and light, strength and wisdom.

Thank you everyone.

-

"But you have to do what you dream of doing even while you're afraid."

-

Arianna Huffington

Mummy, this is for you.
I Miss You.

PROLOGUE

Dude, why do I have to read this book?

Frankly you don't have to, but since you're already reading this page then you bought it already, which could mean that you're either interested enough in what the heck you're supposed to START or you just like me that much.

Either way, it's nice to e-meet you. Haha.

Seriously though, thank you for picking up this strange, strange book.

I hope you love it as much as I do.

I say strange because, I never ever thought, in a million years, I'd write a book.

After a few sessions with my mentor, I think he was definitely convinced I was absolutely crazy, because each time I recounted one of the experiences I have had, in life, in business, he would just sit there dumbfounded, wondering how on earth I am still standing and more importantly, still carrying on.

At least, that was what he told me.

Hope he wasn't lying because his head may end up on a spike, Joffrey Baratheon style.

One day mid session he says, "You know what? You're a little selfish, Jadesola, all these experiences you've had are lessons learnt, and I believe somehow they've helped you in taking your business from where it was to where you are now. You should share them, so you're writing them all down and I need it ready by June".

I looked at this man and thought, someone's blood sugar may be a little low right now because I think he's confusing me with someone else.

I'm not a writer.

But when Yoda speaks you listen, so here we are.

In truth, once I started writing this book I realized truly, how each experience, as awful as some of them seemed at the time, has helped not only with my business, but made me a better person.

Perspectives shift when you get knocked on the side of the head violently by mother universe, while you still have to muscle up the strength to carry on with your tasks.

What you will read in this book are some of the most life changing experiences I have had, and I'm hoping that you can take some lessons from them and adapt them to your own life, your own business.

That, really is what my main hope for you is, after you're done reading my book. (I still can't believe I just said that, my book. Ah! *Dusts off shoulder).

No matter what experiences come your way, I hope you find the strength to pull out the lessons from them. I hope those lessons help you move to a higher state in your life, in your business, and wherever else you need higher vibrations.

Listen, situations will come up where you will be pushed, pushed hard and flat against the most difficult obstacles, the stories in this book are meant to show you that despite everything that will get thrown at you, the best decision you can make for yourself is to start anyway.

Start your journey, step after step, tread your chosen path.

Your only regret in life when the curtain is about to close, is that you never tried.

So start NOW.

Start reading this book. Hehe.

Hope you enjoy it.

XO

Jadesola.

CHAPTER 1

START BEING FLEXIBLE

It used to be very difficult for me to stay unattached once I make a decision, and that directly linked it to any actions I take as a result of that. And so I always make sure I stick to my words. I will do everything to ensure I deliver your job on the day, at the time, promised.

Actions speak louder than words and a person who is able to keep their commitment gets more respect from me than any other person.

On a Tuesday morning, I woke early as usual and set out to tackle a few top priority tasks on my schedule for the day.

This required that I stay in the face (literally), of one of my contractors, to get him to finish off on the project on hand so that I, in turn can deliver to the client on time.

Now, encountering Lagos traffic on any normal day is insane, being stuck in it on a day that you have a deadline is like having Thor's hammer sitting heavy on the wings of your aircraft.

Knowing this, I left my office well in advance to go meet up with this contractor working on the job at his office.

I was almost halfway to my destination when I looked up and I saw it in front of me, the blinking angry red color of brake lights, clearly letting me understand that Thor's hammer is about to land on my plane if I don't make a quick getaway.

I decided to leave my car in a nearby car park and take a bike ride to my destination. This was a great idea if you subtract the fact that my heart nearly jumped out of my chest the entire back ride. I honestly think my bike driver believed he was on the set of one of Tom Cruise's movies.

Anyway, I picked up the work from my worker guy, breathed a sigh of relief and hopped back on the ride with my Tom Cruise.

At this point, I had decided that I'd just use this bike man's service to get all my other tasks done, before I finally head back to my car to drive to my last appointment, that way I'd outsmart that damn Lagos traffic!

All was going great, we were speeding off towards my next appointment when I had a feeling something was amiss, my bag which I carried as a backpack felt a little lighter, so I brought it around to check why that was.

My stomach dropped as soon as I brought it round.

My bag had been slashed and the content missing.

I asked the bike driver to pull over so I could check.

Naturally, the first thing I went to look for was my car keys.

It was gone, along with my wallet and a couple other items in the bag.

"I am phecked", I thought.

This wouldn't be a problem since there should be a spare right?

Nope! The only spare I had was that of the fob for the doors, the ignition keys I had on me that day was my spare, because I had been robbed a year or so prior to this particular day and had lost my master key during that.

I first sat down in confusion, shock, then anger and finally broke down crying when the frustration hit.

The bike man could not look at me, he was embarrassed and so he walked a few steps away (poor guy).

The tears eventually dried (all of 5 mins of solo pity party) and then my brain kicked into overdrive.

The first thing I thought about was, "I still need to make this delivery, my client is leaving town tomorrow and I promised him I'll get the items to him, so how could I do this?"

My list of "power resources" literally flashed in my face.

I picked up my phone, started making calls, reorganizing scheduled appointments and all sorts.

That was it, I was back on the back of my dragon, soaring and about to kick some butt.

For the rest of that day, to make sure that my client was not disappointed, I had to stay with the bike man as my mode of transportation.

It was not cool, but I delivered as promised and client was happy.

He didn't know why my eyes were a little red and I appeared ummm, wind blown.

My takeaway from this experience was that, when things get tough, the tough don't just get going, that's a lie, they cry, they moan, then they get back up and get going.

While you're going through this situation, it's important to acknowledge any emotion that hits you as a result of what's happening and remember; Don't kill anyone!

No, I'm not going to tell you it's not likely to happen to you, one way or the other you will face something like that along the course of running your business, put your big person panties on and take note of these useful tips.

Create a power resource list; think of this as the emergency resource list for your business, it should include names of people that you can call at a second's notice, location of your spare keys, ICE cash and stuffs like that.

Communicate your needs; it's not only about having the power list, you have to know how to get the most out if it, and the one crucial way to do that is via adequate communication.

Remember, you may not have a lot of time (in fact you probably won't), therefore being able to CLEARLY communicate what you need at that time is poignant.

Be flexible enough to consider other options.

CHAPTER 2

START PAYING ATTENTION

There's no better feeling than that of being loved and it doesn't matter whether you share the same bloodline or not.

Thankfully I have been fortunate in my life to have one of such great loves in my life, in the form of my best friend and fellow crazy person - Tola.

I called her up this particular morning to wish her a great day before mine got so busy that I forget (don't judge me, I sometimes forget to eat).

She then mentions to me that she would be around my block as she's coming to a supermarket nearby, so she'll stop over.

Yay, I responded, knowing fully well that could very well mean ice cream from a creamery not too far from us.

She shows up barely half an hour later, but with the 13 yr old girl living with her - Segi.

We didn't want to take her with us as we weren't going to be gone long, so we asked her to wait in the office and told her we'd be back in a jiffy.

My employee at the time - Kamon, was also there engrossed in work. I left him with some instructions on what we were working on and told him that we'd be back in a jiffy.

We left to go get some books (because books wouldn't make us fat hence ditched the ice cream idea) and drove straight back to my office barely an hour later.

I opened the door and we were both chatting cheerfully about the books we just got.

I headed into the workroom with the mind to get back into the work and as I entered Kamon started talking about something, he was so incoherent that I couldn't immediately make out what it was he was trying to tell me.

Somehow, while trying to figure his sudden weirdness out, I looked up and caught Segi's face.

I died a little inside.

I knew something horrible had happened.

I called and asked her to come to me so I could figure out what happened.

As she did, I noticed she was visibly shaking, somewhere in my mind, I said a little prayer to God.

"Please let it be that this boy only attempted to touch her and nothing else. Please, please God", I prayed.

But no he didn't just touch her.

Kamon had raped her.

As I walked her outside, to go talk to her privately, I started to notice the blood on her clothes.

She recounted how this guy had forcefully penetrated her and warned her not to tell anyone, as it would be her word against his.

The first thing I did was run outside to get help from my neighbour, to help detain Kamon while I quickly drove to the police station with Tola to get the police.

As soon as he was taken into custody by the police, (after a long ass process and don't even get me started on Nigerian Police system), we took Segi to the hospital to get her checked out before heading back to the police station.

It was a lot of back and forth, tears, questions, regrets and more tears.

Kamon was arrested, but nothing could ease the pain of the trauma.

First for that poor girl, then Tola who couldn't stop blaming herself for bringing her, and for me as I couldn't stop asking myself how I missed it.

I have had this employee for over a year and worked with him, one on one for the entire time.

Then there was the realization that it could have been me, or that he could have killed the girl, on and on and on.

For the first week after the incident, I couldn't walk into my office. It was just impossible for me not to immediately recoil in horror as soon as I attempted going in.

Then clients started calling for their deliveries and I had to muster up the strength, so I went in.

That was when I saw the blood on the floor.

I got cleaning utilities and proceeded to take care of it but that then set me back another two weeks thereabout where I would just cry, and wonder if anything was worth it at the end of the day.

I couldn't get rid of the regrets, and I had that in many different forms, so much so that I lost my mojo for work.

Somehow, if I wanted my business stay open I had to find the strength to get back up.

❖

Even when you think you have all your bases covered, sometimes you get hit in the face with one of the most incredible challenges it completely knocks you off your feet, and your drive, passion or motivation simply just disappears with it.

Allow yourself that time to process what happened and recover, remember that the only thing you can control is yourself.

Also never ever assume that someone will reason similar to how you think.

When you are down and ask yourself why you should even bother to continue, remember why you started in the first place.

Find a way to restore that passion.

CHAPTER 3

START TAKING RESPONSIBILITY

It'd been 6 months since the Kamon incident and I couldn't begin to describe the amount of disarray my schedule was in.

Kamon was my number one employee, he was the one that had been consistently growing and improving his skills after I trained him up to my acceptable standard for my work.

After his arrest, I needed new employees.

I interviewed a minimum of three new workers, who claimed they could "do anything".

However, I tested them with practical work and they failed miserably.

At some point, I decided that I may just have to train them to my standard, and so with the last recruit I went ahead and started training her.

It was a disaster.

After each lesson, she would "get it" but once I gave her a task I'd quickly realise she had not learnt anything.

My favourite song became "oh Lord Jesus, save me".

It was a colossal waste of time and resources.

Next best strategy was to outsource.

What that meant was, I couldn't keep as tight a watch on the quality of work, as well as time management, as I normally would have done to be productive.

Let me ask you this, have you by any chance seen a headless chicken just flapping around after it's head has been severed off but the thing just won't die?

That was me chasing after these vendors up and down.

It was a real hustle.

The final straw? A huge contract came in from an existing client and I had to outsource a part of it.

Now imagine going through all the aforementioned up and downs with the vendors, and the client calling back a few days later because he wasn't happy with the work.

Client: "This is not the same quality I'm used to from you Jadesola".

Me: "Huh?". Sad face.

It was so demoralising.

All I could think about was, "I cannot refund anyone o, money has gone into the business".

I got scared then angry, "that phecking Kamon of a guy, if he'd kept his thingy in his pants my business process wouldn't have been disrupted".

I also got whiny, "this damn vendor, because I couldn't literally live in his office to monitor the work, look at what has happened"

Then there was the anger at myself, "and you too, becoming so frazzled after all that's happened, that you didn't take enough time to quality check the work before delivering to the client, plus how is it that one employee has so much power to put your business in such disarray?"

Thankfully I came back to my senses, after all that moaning and whining.

I decided to sort this mess out.

"Hmm Option, options, options!". I thought.

I went through about three different scenarios, noted them down and started attacking them one after the other, fully aware that time was running out.

The client did give me some time to correct the mistakes so I was grateful, but then that meant i was, once again, under a lot of additional stress.

After what felt like ages, the craziest thought came to my head.

Head: "You need to call Kamon back to sort this mess out, he's the only one you know that can handle this properly, especially in such short time"

Heart: "Are you insane? He raped someone in your office. What will people think if they find out you worked with him after the incident? What if he attacks you this time instead? How can you forgive such a person?".

Head: "Stop being so damn emotional about things and think about this logically, at this point you're about to be phecked if you don't calm down".

Heart: "You better discuss this with people first".

Head: "I agree".

So I picked up my phone and immediately called my mentor to run him through the situation. I was honestly expecting him to agree with Heart that I'm crazy.

But he didn't. He calmly listened to me and told me that at this point, that's the most logical thing to do.

I called another friend of mine that I know will tell me as it is and not mince words.

He said the same thing.

I called a third person, he didn't like the idea at all, but understood i was boxed in, so agreed that since it was to be for just that single issue, i should take the risk.

After a final lengthy discussion, I decided to consider it.

However, I had a big BUT attached to it.

I had to let my best friend know about this, the initial incident involved us both and we were obviously greatly affected by it.

If she said no or wasn't happy with this decision, I wasn't sure I'd be able to go through with it, because honestly, I truly would rather not.

As she was going on a holiday, I made sure I informed her that same day.

I walked over to her house and told her, she was surprised at first, asked me if I was sure it was a good idea and if I thought it would work.

We talked about it and eventually she said yes.

A day after, I summoned up the courage, called Kamon's Uncle first, to inform him of my plans, before calling Kamon himself.

He promised that Kamon had been dealt with, and he would personally vouch for him for the period of time I needed him.

I called Kamon a couple of hours later, he apologised bla bla, bla. Me? I wasn't in the mood to hear his stupid apologies frankly.

He agreed to come in to work on the pieces so we decided on a date and time.

On the set day, this boy didn't show up as promised, calls after calls, days passed, still no show.

Eventually, I resigned to the fact that he wasn't going to show.

I was secretly relieved to be honest.

He later showed up to my studio after about a week ready to work.

I had never experienced the intensity of some of the emotions I did that day.

At the sight of him, my heart started beating so fast.

I was so scared just seeing him again after the incident, but I managed to remind myself to stay calm and not get triggered.

I needed the work corrected.

"Keep a cool head so you can respond properly if anything happens", I told myself.

Once he was in the workroom, I went to my office to take some deep breaths.

Ooohhhhhsah!!!

After that breathing exercise, I called my mentor to tell him how I was feeling, and then my boyfriend.

I asked him to come over and work at my office for that day so I'm not alone.

It took my him a few hours to get to me, by the time he did, I was a mess.

I couldn't concentrate because each time I turned my back on Kamon, I felt like I was about to get stabbed in the back.

Visions of me scrubbing the bloodstains off the floor, of the girl shaking in my arms as I held her, of my bestie crying and blaming herself, kept flashing like disco lights in my mind.

I was a hot mess.

Kamon must have picked up on that too, because he simply couldn't look me in the eyes.

Neither one of us was getting any work done.

After some hours slow dancing in that burning room, I had to send him away.

I realized that I better call the client to ask for an extension.

I promised him that if I couldn't correct the error I would replace the work, although I cried a little inside while I made that promise.

A week or so after this episode, my bestie got back from holiday all bronzed and gorgeous.

She sent me a message that we needed to have a brief chat, but she was out running errands so would call me later in the evening.

She ended up texting instead, and that message turned my day upside down, inside and out, poured bleach on it and turned my flame to ash.

She had thought about the Kamon working with me again issue and she felt betrayed, hurt and basically disappointed.

She couldn't understand how I could call him back to work after what he did.

A lot of other things were said, as you know, when we are angry or hurt we always link issues together, (women eh? If you nodded to that, stop reading my book right now!)

There was no explanation I could give her at this point, that didn't sound to her like I was being selfish, because she believed I made that decision without considering how she, and the other people involved, felt.

I was annoyed and hurt as well, because I knew I had her consent to go ahead, so how could she say those things?.

Anyway it took some patience, understanding and a lot of love, to work through it and communicate adequately how we each felt so as to resolve the issue.

It wasn't easy, but it was done.

Was it sufficient? Did it make everything okay immediately?

No it didn't.

In fact, I thought I lost her, and that nearly broke me.

After all that, I had to take account of the fall outs from that decision.

The doubts started slowly creeping into my mind.

I was questioning my own decision making abilities, started wondering if everyone that had called me "too emotional" were right after all.

"These advisers of mine, were they right in supporting the idea that I should call a Kamon back for the job rework?"

"Did they even consider the emotional impact that decision would have on me?"

In business, you will need to make different decisions, some will be easy, some will be hard.

Some you will make for the growth of your business, but it may come at the expense of your relationships.

I will never advice you not to make them.

If you do, be prepared to be responsible for those decisions and their consequences.

When you seek advice, remember that the final lock on the key is yours. You decide whether to go ahead or not, not matter what.

Be careful with your expectations, when you do make those difficult decisions, don't go around expecting that the other persons involved "should" understand your reasons.

You need to work on yourself well in advance, and deeply enough, to know that only you are responsible for whatever decisions you make, and the consequences of those decisions.

CHAPTER 4

START TRUSTING

It was Wednesday morning around 6am, I picked up my phone after my shower to call my boyfriend and wish him a good day ahead, and also to make sure he was up and getting ready for his meeting at 7:30am.

The boy can sleep!

Now, why did I need to call him?

Well, by the time I left his place the previous night he was pretty knackered as we'd both had the longest, most stressful day.

Not what you're thinking you disgusting person, hahaha.

Plus he'd told me how important it was for him to attend that meeting, so I took it upon myself to be his wake up call for 6am.

Meh! Over-syllabus kill person.

By 6:10am I had called him twice, he wasn't picking up his phone.

This was was unlike him, therefore I resorted to what I termed intermittent calling.

I'd call his number, then wait between 5 to 7 mins to call back.

6th call, no answer, shet!

I started to panic, all sorts of thoughts were running through my mind.

Was he hurt?

Had he already left but forgot his phone?

No maybe, his battery died.

On and on these thoughts kept coming.

Through all that though, my predominant fear was that he was hurt.

Then out of nowhere, i got hit by a major one.

It was, wait! did he lie to me about this meeting and is secretly doing 'something' else?

"Nope, not gonna happen to me again", my heart told my brain.

That gave me enough reason to have a proper panic attack, so I quickly got dressed and went to his house (which was thankfully about 10 mins walk from mine) to check on him.

You see, we just started dating and I happen to really like this guy, even though I was fighting it so hard while my mentor (that devil) was having a filled day, laughing at me.

As soon as I got to his door, my brain quickly logged a few information.

His car was parked in the usual lot, his lights were on and the AC in his apartment was running, meaning he must be in the house.

Then the knocking started.

Bam, bam, bam, bam………

I didn't get any answer,

Now with my keys, Ko, ko, ko, ko, ko………

Still no answer,

Shet!

I started sweating.

At first my mind was numb, I couldn't think of anything else to do, then I told myself to calm Le pheck down.

"Even if he's in trouble, your fear can't help, think of something productive", I mused.

I remembered he hates any form of heat, once the temperature rises a little, this man gets uncomfortable.

I smiled a little to myself as I cut off his power supply from the main switch, hoping he'll wake up when he starts sweating.

I then set my timer for 5 mins, waiting by the door with my feet tapping some random rhythm.

4 mins and 12 seconds later, his door opens up, he comes outside, sees me and says "Babe, are you okay? What's wrong?"

I felt the most incredible wave of relief course through my body, he was okay.

All was well again in Loveniverse.

I looked up at him standing there and I couldn't even be mad, half asleep and groggy he was HOT so obviously I had to forgive him.

The things we do for love right?

The long story short, he'd just forgotten to set his alarm and so overslept.

After I calmed down and we talked about the situation, an incredible realization hit me, it suddenly dawned on me that somewhere there, I still had a fear of being cheated on.

The reason is, I had had a boyfriend who I caught cheating on me, in the same kind of scenario where I had to rush to his house, to check on him as he was meant to travel that morning, only to find him in bed with another woman.

This was my first love, and you know what they say about firsts, so you can imagine.

More than a decade after that incident, I thought I had gotten over and worked through it, but it got triggered again with this new experience.

It took me a bit to reassess the situation and pull out all the reasons why this scenario is completely different from that previous experience, to get myself out of that unresourceful state.

The thing is, no matter how hard and terrible your previous experience was, you will still have to open the door for a new one.

Use the lesson from the past to create a better outcome for new ones.

A time will come when something will happen and it will take you straight back to that awful experience, you need the clarity of mind and discipline to assess the situation and pull out the differences and the resources that will serve you in a positive way.

When you feel like you're stuck in a situation and there's no way out, just literally tell your mind to be still and give you room to come up with solutions.

They are all there from all your past experiences and encounters it's just a matter of pulling up a useful one for that moment.

CHAPTER 5

START LISTENING

It was around 1pm on this bright and glorious day in what you may call downtown Lagos, also known as Balogun Market.

I was on my way out of the busy market heading back to my studio. I had to go finish up some of the work I had on hand as my main equipment broke down and this was the only other alternative I could think of at that point.

I had two sewing machines, a lot of other gadgets, 9 bridesmaids dresses and the bride's dress herself in the car with me that day.

I wasn't going home until I got a solution.

All was looking great, as everything was done in time for the last fitting before I'd have to do the finishing touches then deliver to the client.

The only annoyance on this particular day, at that particular moment, was traffic.

Yes, THE LAGOS TRAFFIC.

I had been the sitting duck behind the wheel for about 45 mins at this point, and from passers by I understood the cause to be that some politicians were around the area campaigning, it was about a month or to the presidential elections.

Thankfully, I had Michael Jackson belting out "the way you make me feel", I had Coke Zero in my hand,

I was prepared for battle.

"We will stay here and fight this crazy traffic through till the end", I kept repeating to myself.

Who was I fooling, it wasn't like I could go anywhere anyway, we were stuck, but it made me feel good to think that way.

I was consoling myself when I spotted, first, about three cars ahead of me the driver suddenly flung the door open and jumped out, then the car behind that.

It felt as if time suddenly slowed all the way down as I watched in horror, the window of the driver's side, of the car immediately in front of me got smashed in, by a guy that I had thought was just walking past.

The maniac pulled the driver, a woman, out of her car and stabbed her in the shoulder.

"Pheck, pheck!", my mind started racing.

I unlocked my door, turned off the ignition and reached for the door.

But I was too late.

To my right were two angry looking idiots, to the left another two.

They didn't look like they came to ask for lunch money nicely.

My self preservation mode immediately got activated.

I slowly raised both hands in surrender, letting them know I wasn't about to struggle.

Because, me? I did not want to get stabbed.

While my mind was racing and heart pumping like an overworked V12 engine, I suddenly felt someone grab my neck from behind, he pulled the back of my head to my seat's headrest so violently I thought I lost my brain.

That idiot then started yanking, yes, yank - as in forcefully, pull my jewellery off my ears, neck, wherever they saw anything they liked.

The other idiot too, following in his criminal friend/ mentor's footsteps started pulling my watch, rings whatever they could take.

In the back seat they took the bag containing the clothes, the machines I had taken with me to repair, my handbag with all the contents and even my half consumed bottle of coke.

Yes, they must have been hungry.

Motherpheckers!

Once they were satisfied, they left me and ran off.

I was glued to my seat, fear wouldn't let me move.

I must have been like that for a good 5 mins or so, at least it felt like that, before I raised my head.

I saw the passengers in the commercial bus next to me, slowly raising their heads from where they were all hunched over hiding.

My first thought was "so none of you could come down to help me?", but just as quickly another thought came to me asking, "why should they risk their lives to help you?"

Anyway, there was nothing to do but sit, STILL stuck in that traffic for what seemed like eternity (about 20mins or so after the incident).

Once the traffic started easing and cars started to move I put my car in gear and started driving.

I didn't realise how badly I had been hurt until I got to the toll gate and I didn't have any money.

I had to get out of the car to ask a traffic warden for some money.

It was her scream when she saw me that jolted me back to the reality of what had happened.

I had blood dripping from my ears and wrist, bruises on my neck and shoulders and blouse was torn down the front.

She gave me some money, bless her, and I got back in my car, continued driving.

Eventually, I found myself in front of my brother's house, because my house keys were in my bag and those criminals had it.

I had to wait for him to get back from work. It was so hopeless I didn't even have a phone to call anyone.

It was a long ass wait.

❖

So many things I took away from that incident, first of which was that you have to learn to adapt to your environment and whatever situation you find yourself.

See I had just moved back home from the UK and had not done sufficient research on dos and don'ts of going to the market.

I was sitting in my car all dressed up looking fancy and shet.

In my defence, I basically ran out of my studio to go finish up in the market.

I was such an easy target.

There were cars besides mine they didn't attack, possibly because the passengers didn't look like JJC.

Secondly, follow your GUT.

That first reaction or emotion you get when something happens, listen to it.

If I had not listened to my gut which basically said, "Jadesola don't struggle, we don't want to die here this afternoon", I probably would have tried to come up with some Tom Cruise moves to try and escape.

Third thing I learnt is that, practice not only makes perfect, sometimes it bloody well might just save you.

As ridiculous as it may sound, because I got so good at driving to my Brother's house, even while still in shock and clearly not thinking straight, somehow I found myself parked at his gate, waiting for him to return from work.

This for me is the most important lesson.

If you keep practicing, doing something over and over again, it becomes a habit, and on occasions where your life may depend on it, it will come to you "naturally".

CHAPTER 6

START DEVELOPING A SUPER BEESH SENSOR

I basically put my own life in danger because I was desperate.

About two months after I decided to go full throttle on my business, I got a referral from one of my existing clients.

It was so juicy I literally squealed with joy (no I meant roared, dragons don't squeal *Rolling my eyes).

I had just quit my 9 to 5 job in oil and gas you see, so any new referral was like being offered a drop of water when you're stranded in a desert.

Mrs. Bonny was a great client of mine and she always promised to bring me clients.

As a result, when she called to inform me that fateful day, she was on her way to my studio with a new client, I did a happy dance.

She came in with the new client, whom I will refer to as Mrs. M.

Man, just thinking about it now, I have goosebumps.

She already had her fabrics, with her phone loaded with pictures of all the outfits she wanted made.

Before I could catch my breath, she pulled up a chair, opened up her bag and brought out a pack of cigarettes and her lighter.

Now, let me paint you a picture of Mrs. M.

She is a sixty something year old woman, who had relocated from eastern part of Nigeria to "the abroad" where, according to her, she had lived for over 20 years and counting.

Listen, if you've ever had the opportunity to go live in another country outside Nigeria, you'd want to denounce this country too.

On many occasions, it'd seemed to even me, that Nigeria is just happiness intolerant.

Back to my story, Mrs. M was perched on a seat in my studio, about to start smoking, surrounded by patterns (paper form), fabric, wooden furniture and all sorts of sewing equipments, I (nicely) asked her to step outside if she's desperate for her puff of poison.

Deciding it could wait, she put it back in her bag and we started discussions on what she wanted and how she wanted it done after which I explained my processes to her.

Let me ask you something, have you ever had a client who felt like they knew more about your business than you actually do?

I mean those ones that say shet like, "ah ah, is it not just to do this and do that? It's easy now".

She was slowly unraveling to me as one of those people.

Still, I refused to listen to my gut feeling, my poor fairy godmother who was at that point, probably floating around my head in a frenzy while attempting to slap some sense into me.

I refused o, I did not listen.

I wanted Mrs. M's business real bad.

That went on for a bit, eventually, we decided on her styles, fabrics for each style and accessories.

Finally, I gave her, her bill.

"I will send you an official invoice later today. Once you confirm all the details and pay the required deposit I would start", I explained to her.

I sincerely thanked Aunty Bonny (my very good client that brought her) on their way out, breathed a sigh of relief as I shut my door and went back to work.

I was super happy because it was a big invoice, I really needed the money at that point.

(Truth be told, as an entrepreneur when do you never "need that money so bad?).

I sent her the invoice just before my COB as promised, ensuring that I attached all the sketches of the outfits she had agreed to, with pictures of the corresponding fabric for each style.

Mrs. M called me 3 days after her visit to my studio, 3 days after I sent her the invoice.

She was irate, she sounded so angry I could have sworn she had fumes coming out of her ears and mouth, I mean this woman was screeching.

Why you ask?

Well........

"Ehhhnnnn Bolaji or what do they call you, what is this nonsense 5% VAT you have attached to my bill ehh? This is Nigeria o, what rubbish. I'm not paying that so you better take it off my invoice now". She screamed on the phone.

I was just flabbergasted. Like, wait, what?

You know that little voice in your head that calmly reminds you, "you need this money at this point so better take a chill pill?"

Mine reminded me and I listened. I took the phecking chill pill and swallowed the cup too.

I proceeded to explain to this madam that yes, this is not "the abroad", it's Nigeria. My business is registered as an Ltd so by law I have to pay VAT on every sale.

She started screaming again.

"Lie!!! My other tailor in Anambra doesn't charge me any stupid VAT. Take it off or else I'm not going to pay it".

Then she adds, "anyway I have given Bonny some cash to give you, that's my deposit, when I return from the village we will sort this out".

I was about to start my VAT campaign again, to let her know that I need her consent on it, but she hung up.

At this point, I just wanted to slap someone.

I thought the best strategy was to let her friend know about the situation, as a result, I emailed the invoice to Aunty Bonny too, then called her to also explain the situation to her.

She apologised on Mrs. M's behalf and told me to proceed, that she'd talk to her.

The agreement was that her order of about 12 outfits, will be ready in 3 weeks after her deposit.

She was okay with this arrangement, as it'd be just in time for her departure to "the abroad".

Imagine my irritation when this woman started to bother me, barely 10 days into the work, with calls.

She wanted to see them.

"Lay them on the table and take pictures, send them to my WhatsApp, now!. Put them on the hangers too, so I can see the shape".

To each of these ridiculous requests, I would explain that garments don't work that way.

"I can send you pictures but it won't give a true idea of the fit. You'd need to come in and try them on". I explained to her.

Every normal earthling knows this.

Nope.

Mrs. M clearly came from another planet.

Eventually, she came back into Lagos from her village and called that I send the clothes to her.

I reminded her again to come in for fitting, to which she once more refused.

I was like, "well then, have it your way", I was only too happy to be done with her so I sent the clothes via dispatch.

She called me the following morning going mad.

I thought maybe there was something wrong with the clothes after she tried them on, was almost in a panic, but then paused to ask myself, "wait o, did she try even them on?".

Me: "Have you tried the clothes on ma'am?"
Mrs. M: "No, they are here, laid on the table and they won't fit, plus these are not the styles I asked for".

Yes, should I pause here so you can exhale that sharp gasp of outrage you just took on my behalf?

Yes, Breathe!

I thought, "Chai! I have entered this one".

That's how the war started, there was no name she didn't call me.

Thief.

Idiot.

Poor idiot.

Fool.

Illiterate.

I mean, she went on and on, it was trail of expletives left on my already sore track.

At a point I actually hung up on her, I couldn't take it anymore.

Then she started hounding me with calls, she'd call as early as 6am and start her tirade.

Cursing and name calling, having a fit and basically just being a witch.

After a few more of those nasty calls, I called her friend to ask if she could get Mrs. M to try the clothes on, she said she'd try.

To my surprise, Mrs. M called me later the same day, she had tried one of the clothes and actually liked it.

Still, she refused to try any other one as "they are not the styles she had in mind".

By now, I was totally pissed.

I retorted with, "well of course not, I didn't make what you had in mind, I made what we agreed on".

Aunty Bonny later told me she'd talked with Mrs. M, she wanted a full refund and after that, she wants me to replace all her fabrics.

See, when I'm wrong I'm quite happy to rectify the situation and make amends. If I'm not though, maybe God may succeed in changing my mind, because no human on this earth will.

I called to update Aunty Bonny, and she confirmed she had seen the clothes.

The finishing was great, the styles were great, just that Madam won't try them on since she already decided the styles weren't what she asked for.

To which in my mind I replied, "old beesh!".

She sent the clothes, except for the one she liked, back to me. She didn't want them anymore.

I packed them up and kept them.

"When you're ready, you'll come and get your stuff", I told myself.

That was where we left the situation, she went back to her planet.

This happened around September or so.

By August the following year, yes you read that right, the following phecking year.

She was back in town and wanted her money, so the "case" was reopened.

Back and forth, as before, calls were flying so fast you didn't have enough time to blink.

Eventually, her friend convinced her to let me bring the clothes by her place.

She could try them on while I was there so hopefully we'd be able to resolve the issue.

When her friend told me this, I let her know that I wasn't comfortable going to see Mrs. M at her place, because the last time they came to my studio she was throwing things in a fit of rage and actually broke some items.

Aunty Bonny assured me that nothing of that sort will happen.

"I spoke to her, she's a lot calmer now", Aunty Bonny said to me on the phone.

As I parked on the side street near Mrs. M's place (she was staying with another friend) I decided to let Aunty. Bonny know that I was there.

Aunty B: "Oh great, just go in and be calm okay?"

Me: "Yes ma".

Aunty B: "Are you there alone?"

Me: "Yes, I am"

There was a brief pause on her end of the phone before she said, "you should have gone with someone o".

This made the hairs on the back of my neck stand up.

"Oh really?" I quipped.

"Oh it's nothing, just sometimes it's good to have a witness, you know", she replied.

I got worried for a second about what she was insinuating, but I didn't want to assume so I asked her outrightly if she thought I might be in danger.

"Of course not, M is an old woman", she assured me.

So I went to the gate and knocked.

Mrs. M came to open the gate, herself, super friendly and nice.

I thought to myself, "well, well. Maybe she got some new jewellery or she got laid. LOL. Either way, thank you, Jesus."

She took me into the room she was staying in and started smoking immediately.

I really don't enjoy having to deal with second hand smoking but at this point I just chilled.

With a smile plastered across my face, I brought the clothes out .

"Here are the outfits ma'am, I can excuse you to try them on", I said to her.

"What's all this, I was expecting my money", Mrs. M replied.

I was getting annoyed all over again but calmed myself. I pleaded with her, to at least try them on.

She got up, dashed to the door, and I thought she had finally agreed to do the fitting.

Nope.

She locked the door and put the key in her bra.

Shet!

I didn't have time to process what was happening beyond the fact that she was coming at me.

She lunged at me and grabbed my handbag, pulled my T-shirt at the neck (what Nigerians refer to as Lock Your Shirt) and started poking me with her cigarette.

Whether she forgot that it was lit or she was just plain evil, I didn't know, all I remember is screaming, "this is not right, you have no right to attack me, let me out!"

I was screaming so loudly that one of the other occupants of the house came banging on the door, ordering her to open the door.

5 more minutes of this other woman banging the door, and me screaming, the devil briefly left her and she opened the door.

As soon as she let go of me, I made a beeline for my phone, which had fallen during all the drama.

My bag in my hand, I ducked behind her and dashed out the door. By God, Usain Bolt had nothing on me.

I was so scared I felt my legs would not hold me up.

With trembling fingers, I managed to unlock my phone, called my brother to come get me and then broke down in tears once safely outside the compound.

My brother came as fast as humanly possible and we all ended up at the police station.

I had bruises all over and I had cigarette burns right through my T-shirt in the middle of my chest.

This old beesh was trying stop me from wearing cleavage revealing clothes, but the Devil is a liar!!

See ehn? Desperation is an awful thing.

What's even more terrifying are the choices we make, day in day out, without ever being conscious of the repercussions of those decisions.

I needed the money, so I made the choice to take this client despite all the telltale signs, pointing to the fact that it wouldn't end well.

Right from first attempted smoking incident in my studio, I knew she was trouble, but I wasn't willing to look deeper into the well to assess the kind of trouble I was fishing for.

If I had not taken her on, I wouldn't ever have had to tell the story of the cigarette burn marks on my chest.

But then on the flip side, you wouldn't be here reading this while thinking, pheck it, this girl is a dragon.

You know that Celine Dion song "Think twice"?

Go read the lyrics and apply it to your business.

Now flip the page.

CHAPTER 7

START LETTING GO OF INSECURITY

I met this super amazing woman Ibidunni at a training I was attending and we connected immediately.

We had so much in common it was actually ridiculous (in a good way).

One of those turned out to be the love of exercise.

Actually, my mentor, who happened to be friends with her as well, had spoken to her at length about how I love working out and how he hates me for it.

He told her about how I would run 15km distance on the spot because I didn't want to go on the street so early in the morning to run alone.

Need I say that all Ibidunni took from that was the running on the spot bit.

(If you've never done it, I suggest you give it a go. You'll thank me for it later).

Anyway, we were deep in conversation with me going on about how tired I was, after completing my planned 5km run that morning, even though my body was seriously protesting.

Suddenly she went, "Jadesola, hold on, we can't be friends anymore. This running on the spot thing is insane, you're making the rest of us look bad".

I bursted out laughing, "unfortunately for you, you are stuck with me now", I said.

We went back and forth, with me trying to convince her it's not as bad as my mentor made it seem and that we should actually go running together the coming Saturday.

The date was set for Saturday, and as the conversation went on she casually mentioned, "oh I'll just tell some of my friends to join us, KH, will especially love it. She's like you when it comes to exercising. You're both insane".

"Oh awesome, I can't wait" I replied and left it at that.

About two days after, my mentor (that sneaky man), goes, "Oh by the way, Jadesola, you know which KH Ibidunni was referring to?"

I shook my head no.

Again, my mentor (that sneaky man), took a deep breath, looked me dead in the eyes and said, "KH" (can't tell you her full name you may just pass out).

Listen, as far as I'm concerned that woman is a legend, as an actress, as a philanthropist, as a gorgeous human being, I have wanted to meet her since the year B.C, no scratch that, I NEEDED to meet her so bad.

She is just an incredible person and so to hear that I was going to meet her, was beyond amazing.

I couldn't stop thinking about how super cool I was going to TRY to play it and not fangirl too much.

LIE!!

The morning of the race, I picked up Ibidunni and headed to the meet up point.

One by one, all the ladies started showing up. I had never felt so strong and powerful being with a group of women.

Each one of them had such beautiful energies, you could just feel their confidence and personal powers radiate through.

And theeeeennnnnn, she pulled up.

KH, of house H, first of her name, breaker of chains, queen of Nollywood, freaking pulled up.

Oh boy, I kept saying to myself, "be cool, you better be cool Jadesola, dammit!"

She sauntered round to where the rest of us were standing and said hello to everyone, cool as a cucumber, looking super pretty in her workout gear and with the most radiant smile on her face.

As the only newbie, I was introduced to her, she smiled sweetly and said "nice to meet you, Jadesola. So guys, are you ready?"

I was like "damn, she cool".

That's how the race started sha, two seconds into it we had left about 6 strong ass women behind.

ROFL.

We carried on that way for a while, I made it my mission to stay behind her and let her pace lead mine.

Me that I had a plan, I was waiting for the right time to engage her in a conversation, I Knew "dusting" her or running ahead would just have been plain stupid in terms of strategy.

We continued like that for about 3km and eventually I had to get ahead of her.

Listen I had to okay? Deal with it.

So, bam, bam, bam, we carried on, with her just about 2 steps behind me and me silently saying, "ah ah, mama catch up "biko", I need to "famzie" with you some more".

And then the good Lord answered my prayers, she stepped up right beside me as we fell into the most perfect rhythm, steps, breathing, and pace.

It was great.

A couple of times we would just look at each other to decide whether to increase pace or slow down a bit, to catch our breaths.

I'm telling you, it was beautiful to watch.

We decided to power walk to rest a bit rather than stopping completely, at some point, we were both getting tired (around 9km already).

And that's how she turns to me and asked, "are you okay?"

Pppffffwwwwwwooooooosssshhhhhhh!!

My heart exploded inside my chest.

I thought, "Pheck YEAHHHHH" but I kept it cool and just smiled, "yes ma'am, thank you", I replied.

She laughed at the "ma'am" bit, then started conversation like it was nothing.

We talked about everything, people's mindsets about health and fitness, the country's attitude towards it, how we can help, what we can do, I mean everything.

We ended up doing 12km in total that morning. It was incredible.

That woman, she would cheer herself after each kilometer, yelling "whooooop" at each milestone.

She didn't need anyone to do it for her, she was in tune and grounded enough in herself.

For a superstar celebrity, she was so comfortable in her own skin, all sweaty and barefaced and she still found time to holla and yell "you can do it" to other runners on the road.

Some inspirational shet right there, I tell ya.

You, that you have one small Mercedes Benz in your compound, you will be pressing accelerator, zoom zoom zoom, all the time and not allow people rest.

"See your life outside".

Anyway back to my aunty KH (yes I am claiming her as my aunty).

At the end of the race I thanked her for such a great experience, because in truth it was just that, a great run at a great pace with amazing women.

"Actually, no darling, I should thank you, I have never done a 5:58 mins/km before, I was following you, your pace controlled mine", she replied.

For the second time that day, my mind was blown. I wasn't sure I heard her correctly.

Was that a compliment? From KH? To me?.

I smiled politely, we took pictures with the whole group. She even did some videos for her social media and made sure to tag everyone (yes, she asked for mine too).

See, all these didn't mean anything to me, until I got home and I started thinking back on it.

I came to an incredible understanding that, as excited as I was to meet her, I had a lot of insecurities.

Will she like me?

Would I be good enough?

I mean she's a superstar for freaking sake, and these other women are amazing and super successful, why would she want to interact with a nobody like me?

To then go from that state and end up hearing that I was more than enough, I was capable and she absolutely liked me, enough to give me her personal number, was a moment I'll always come back to whenever I need a pick up or morale boost.

Never allow doubt and insecurities to stop you from stepping out and trying something new with someone new.

CHAPTER 8

START PERFORMING THOUGHT
SURGERIES ON YOURSELF

Have you ever met someone, you take one look at them and you just knew you were kindred spirits?

Not the sappy love at first sight type, but the one where you just knew this person was as naughty, cool, intense and kind as you are.

(Yes I'm all that and more, if you doubt that well blame your creator lol).

This was the case when I met Akanji, I had an appointment to go measure him as a referral from one of my existing clients.

He buzzed me in as soon as I let him know I was downstairs in the lobby of the hotel he was staying at.

I walked in and took a quick scan of his room, it was in ummm, what I refer to as a situation, as he had a "guest".

In truth, it was none of my business, but I couldn't resist a knowing smirk.

"Boys will always be boys", I mused to myself.

He must have noticed that smirk or it must have been that I wasn't discreet enough, because he turned around from what he was doing and caught me.

That was the moment I knew we would be friends for ever.

We both smirked as I walked to the seat he offered me.

It took him about 5 mins or so to clear his space and tell his guest, "I'll call you later".

That was okay as far as I was concerned, it afforded me time to set up my equipments and bring out my notepad to start the session.

As he lowered himself into his seat, he looked at me with a challenging smirk and asked, "what did you see?"

I looked straight back at him, with a silent challenge of my own and responded, "exactly what you weren't prepared for me to see".

We both bursted out laughing and when we finally caught our breaths he said, "you are so phecking mischievous".

From that point, we talked about everything and anything, our mutual love for F1 and LH44 (if you know, you know) to fashion and runway shows.

It was an interesting conversation and he was an intriguing guy.

We eventually got around to the session and as I was leaving he said to me in that same mischievous tone, "you better phecking keep in touch outside of business".

And this was how the friendship started.

We were always chatting about so many things, current affairs, the economy, movies, family, spirituality, our values and goals in life.

The conversations were easy and fun.

It was during one of these conversations I found out, that he'd been separated from his wife for about two years and was only casually dating. I mentioned to him I had been single for about 2 years.

"Oh my God, don't you ever get horny, or you prefer self help?" He exclaimed.

I don't need to tell you where that conversation ended because he was just a silly goat.

Lol

We became really great friends and somehow along the line it seemed to me, it was progressing to something a little more.

Once in a while I'd test the "situation" with a well placed question, which he would easily answer and consequently set my butt even more firmly in the "I may be falling in love with this man" concrete I had mixed up for myself.

One day I suddenly noticed that after his return journey back from home, he seemed a little off.

He was talking a lot more about his estranged wife and his kids.

He was always talking about his kids anyway, you could tell how much he absolutely loves them, but once he started talking a lot more about his ex I knew it was time to put my big girl panties on and ask a direct question.

Before I summoned enough courage though, mid conversation with him a day or so later, he casually mentions how they had decided to move back in together.

"We may actually be relocating to the Ghana to ease the strain of separation caused by my work", he said.

I immediately put my game face on and went, "oh wow, that's amazing, so you guys worked it out then?".

Obviously, he knew me quite a bit at this point, so he just went....

"Khalisee, I have to do this for my kids, for my family, that's why I didn't give any concrete answer or try to make any moves with you. I really like you but that's all there can be".

I smiled and told him not to be silly, that all was fine and I would talk to him later.

I made sure I hung out with him for like an additional half hour thereabouts, just to make sure I secured my cool factor before leaving.

Silly me.

I got home, called my mentor and had a lengthy discussion with him, aka whined and moaned about how life was so phecking unfair, why can't anything nice happen for me, bla bla, bla, I finally met a great guy and he won't stay.

You know the usual pity party shet.

SMH!

He listened, but allowed me be my own judge and jury. When I was done ranting, he still stayed silent, waited patiently for me to have my aha moment.

"Is it possible that I blew this whole thing up and this grand friendship and possibly love was all in my own head?", I asked him.

His response was that I should open up my heart, and be honest enough with myself to dissect the situation.

"Jadesola, only you have the answer, because no one else felt what you felt, saw what you saw or heard what you heard", he said.

I had allowed this situation to get to that point all on my own, without carefully checking all the facts.

A lot of times we get so wrapped up in a situation, that we completely ignore or possibly forget that there's always another side to it.

There are always the subtle signs that, because we don't pay attention to them, we mostly end up getting lost.

You may have bright ideas but if you don't find a way to rationally dissect what's going on, you may find yourself in trouble.

It's imperative that you start (this second) to pay attention to your thoughts, signs and happenings around you.

These are your unique maps to your next destination.

CHAPTER 9

START LIVING IN THE MOMENT

July 9th, 2017 was one of those days in Lagos where, unless you were there to witness the kind of torrential rain that fell, you'd probably think whoever was telling you the story was making shet up.

It had been raining consistently for two days prior and the roads were filling up with water.

One of the major issues in Lagos state is inadequate drainage system, for a city with majority of its population on an island, you can imagine the kind of disaster that could result in.

People's homes were filled, cars were floating and it got so bad some people had kayaks on the streets of Lagos to move about.

My case was extra special, I was moving into a new house which I sadly found out that, was basically just built for dry season only.

Why, you ask?

Well, with the rain pouring, shet started to blow, roofs were falling down and doors were coming off at the hinges.

The water system wasn't working properly and the ones that were, needed cleaning.

The house wasn't connected to power grid yet and the agent I had gone through to get the house was nowhere to be found.

I had been on the phone with my mum, about two times a day at the minimum throughout that whole process, trying to get advice and mostly support really, because I was going mad.

My mum, was like a ray of sunshine on the cloudiest day, she was the voice of reason and the soothing balm when you feel your soul would to explode.

She was a warrior, feisty, strong, confident, hard working and most importantly, a person capable of loving like you have never experienced.

Right from my younger years I never knew her to be anything other than loving, supportive, strict when needed and just an overall badass.

I am the fourth child of five, the last of two girls.

Every single one of my siblings, was a wonderful alien in my eyes, talented, brave and insanely cool.

My oldest brother, I believe came out of my mother's womb as some form of shrink. Lol

He was always so calm, reasonable and ridiculously funny. He would make us laugh days on end, telling jokes and stories of all his escapades.

My sister; the only one I have, is basically a living and breathing encyclopedia. She is super smart with a great mind for coming up with incredible ideas. She is, (possibly will always be, despite being a successful Doctor) a born hustler with an astounding knack for coming up with business ideas.

One of my brothers could make pencil sketches like you've never seen, he taught himself to play the piano and then the guitar. Once he decided he liked something, he would learn it.

The other followed in his footsteps too, with the music and musical instruments, he was just as talented.

Me on the other hand, I felt like an alien, I couldn't draw much, I wasn't coming up with business ideas, I loved (still do actually), reading.

Mostly though, I only wanted to create something, with my bare hands, you know like build something.

But, I was a very shy, highly introverted child.

I didn't know what any of these meant until adulthood.

I remember as far back as maybe 6 or 7 years old, wondering if something was wrong with me.

I had woken up super happy and cheerful one day, ready to go play either football or wrestling with my brothers. (Yes, I was a tomboy and I loved it).

But someone had sent me to go bring them a plate from the kitchen.

At the time, we lived in a house full of people.

My mum had five of us while also raising about 20 other people from my our extended family.

Yep, again she was a real life angel.

I went into the small kitchen at the rear end of the house, two of my aunties were there cooking.

As soon as I entered something hit me, not physically but I felt this sudden rush of emotion that I couldn't place.

I was suddenly so annoyed, then immediately became sad, for no reason I burst into tears.

Both of them looked up at me for some seconds.

One asked "what's wrong with you now?", turned to the other and said "she's always crying and emotional".

These said in my native language of Yoruba.

I left (with the plate of course, otherwise my little behind would have received some smacking), and went to sit alone at some corner, wrestling forgotten, sad and in a mood for reasons I couldn't explain.

So many more incidents would happen like that, where I'd suddenly get emotional, my mood would change and I could neither explain why nor control it.

I'd come in contact with a group and suddenly my mood will change based on that of the group.

It wasn't just negative emotions, it was positive ones sometimes too.

Each time it happened, someone would make a comment along the lines of "why are you so emotional, so soft? It's not a good thing o, you have to toughen up".

Another one of those occasions was at my 21st birthday party, my sister had planned a surprise party, made me come home from school on some cooked up story, which I later discovered to be a lie.

At 21 years of age I already knew I didn't like large crowds or anything that was going to create an intense emotional cloud, I just still didn't quite know why.

The party was going along nicely when bam! Suddenly, power went off.

Black out.

It was raining heavily outside, all we could do was light lamps and wait for the power to come back up.

Guests were getting anxious, some complaining they had not eaten, moods were rapidly shifting.

As my nature, I started soaking all that up and getting upset too.

Long story short, I cried all through that party and nobody knew why.

No, actually they thought I was upset because "my party wasn't going so well".

Ppfffff.

They knew nothing, Jon Snows.

At some point I must have gone into my room to hide, because my mum found me there.

She asked what was wrong but I couldn't tell her exactly what. She sat with me for a while, looked me dead in the eye and said "never ever feel sorry for who you are and what you are, you are special, you are rare and you are a gift, what you need to do is learn to embrace that and use it to your advantage".

Me? I was just looking at this woman like, "Mummy, what in the blazes are you talking about now, I don't like this large crowd and all the fussing that you people have going on, that's why I'm a little upset". She smiled and nodded.

That moment though, was when I knew that my mum knew more about me than she was letting on, she knew something about me that I didn't and I promised myself I'd hound her till she told me.

From then on, we developed an incredible bond.

Not that we didn't have one before, but she became the only person I could show my real feelings to, that i didn't feel like I needed to "toughen up" and pretend with her.

Each time i had one of my episodes, I would call her, she'd tell me stories about what I was going through and how her dad had similar experiences, she'd try to explain to me the best she could and told me to just embrace it.

She said to me one day "you have to learn about your gift, love it and use it to help yourself and others".

"Mummy, what gift? This can't be a gift when I always seem weak compared to others", I'd sometimes retort.

At the back of my mind though, "I need to figure out what this was", I promised myself.

So back to July 9th 2017, I had spoken to her at length about the issues with the house, in fact I wanted to go visit her because she wasn't living in the same city that I was, but she advised me to wait until I was done with the move and the house issues sorted.

She reminded me that agents and workers were notorious for disappearing after they get paid, "try to pin them down and have the house sorted first, then you can come", she advised.

It was a long, intense and tiring day , still, by 8:45pm I was back on the phone with her making plans for the decor and catching up, like she always loved.

Previously, she'd randomly call me up and say "Bonje, Báwo ni? Óyá gist me now, what's been happening?" To which I would reply, Mummy we spoke this morning.

Lol.

9:23pm we said our good nights and our customary "I love you".

She had a way of singing it, rather than just saying and it always made me laugh.

Monday morning, July 10th, I woke up and went through my usual routine, work out, shower, dress up and head into work.

I remember exactly choosing to wear a white shirt I had stolen from my baby brother and a pair of men's trousers I had made for myself.

White on grey with electric blue pump for a pop of color.

I was ready to take on the day.

The first call I got was from that foolish Landlord's lawyer, I was still having issues with the house and because I refused to pay him his own cut of 10% of my rent as his legal fees, he was hounding me with calls.

I heard my phone beep while I was on the phone with him and I made a mental note to call the person back.

As soon as I ended the call with him though, my sister in law's call came in.

"Hey sis, good morning. What's up?", I said.

She replied in one of the calmest, steadiest tones I have possibly ever heard from her.

"Have you spoke to your brother?"

My stomach immediately dropped as I asked her, "what's wrong, is he okay? Are the kids okay?"
****

Actually I'm going through those feelings again right now as I'm writing this, I'm going to stop here and come back to it.

****

She said all was well, but my brother was heading to Ibadan (my parents lived there at the time) and that I should call him.

"Okay, I'll do that now. Thanks", I quickly hung up.

"Hello D, good morning, Ed said I should call you. What's going on, are you okay? Why are you going to Ibadan?", I bombarded him with questions.

He said he was fine but mummy had a fainting spell, as a result he wants to go there and make sure she's okay.

"Hmmm, something is not right here" I thought.

Daddy is there and he's in the medical profession, my oldest brother is there, so between the two of them I'm sure mummy is in great hands.

Now don't get me wrong, we would all have gone there eventually, but my brother had to cancel an international trip scheduled for that morning.

If it wasn't a serious issue he would have just hounded Dad and my brother to make sure she got the best care until he returns.

Anyway, something was off, I had "the butterflies", (I usually have two types and this wasn't the good one), so I decided to call my dad.

By the time I hung up the call with D, my dad had called me like 4 times already.

"Oh God", I muttered.

That was when I knew.

He answered the phone and let out the biggest wail/scream.

"She's gone, she's gone, it's your mummy. She's gone"!

I swear, as I'm typing this I feel slightly dizzy and my stomach is flipping.

All I remembered was screaming NO, so loudly.

My assistant at the time rushed in to find out what had happened.

I was sitting on the floor, rocking back and forth and whispering "no, it's not true", over and over again into the phone.

"NO! it's not possible, she can't be gone, she was fine last night, Daddy please tell me it's not true".

Someone must have taken the phone from him because the line went dead.

I immediately called my brother back, he was super calm and was kept saying "I know Jadesola, try and breathe, I wanted to get there first before telling you".

I was broken.

NO.

I was shattered into tiny pieces.

My entire world, my support, my angel, my hero, was gone.

I didn't want to believe it, but it was true.

It took us another 4 hours or so to travel from our city to my family's residence .

What I saw when I got there, is something that I will never, ever get over.

I went over to her, laid down beside her and started whispering in her ear, begging her to wake up, that I wasn't ready for her to be gone.

"I can't be me without you Mummy, please wake up, please Mummy I need you".

But she didn't wake up.

She was gone.

My mother was dead.

I would love to tell you that the events after that were all a blur, that I can't remember any of it.

But that wouldn't be true.

I remember exactly all I had to do, and say, throughout that day.

I remember how sad, then angry, then empty I felt.

I remember with clarity, how I'd look into some persons eyes and immediately feel their emotions too.

I remember exactly how drained I felt the morning after.

I remember how empty I still feel, till today.

It's been a little while now, and despite all the countless (foolish and inconsiderate) "you have to move on, don't cry, don't dwell on the sadness" advices, time hasn't healed anything.

If anything, it has caused me to look deeper into this thing we call reason.

"You are my reason to be this, you are my reason to be that".

It's good to know that someone believes in you, but if that's your only motivation, then you're going to be phecked when they leave (because everyone leaves eventually one way or the other).

I have come to understand that if your reason for anything in your life, is attached to sources outside of yourself, you may have issues forging ahead, when that reason leaves.

Sure, part of your why should be because, you want to make someone proud, make an impact in someone else's life, leave your mark and so on.

All of that has to circle back and become centered around making a mark in YOUR own life.

Everything happens for a reason, guess what? You are that reason.

Be the reason that you wake up each day and start the race towards your goals.

CHAPTER 10

START IGNORING COPYCATS

I hired a media lady I was working with when I first got back to Nigeria.

I really didn't want to, I didn't feel like I needed one yet as my brand was still budding.

Everyone however, told me I needed visibility on social media, that "most fashion brands just hire PR people to take care of that for them".

So even though I was broke all the damn time, I squeezed myself and signed up with this PR agency.

She would help me get Magazine features, create relationships with celebrities and find stockists, as well as collaborators for my brand, in a bid to sha get known fast o.

Yeah, such schemes usually just backfire, I realised that later on though.

At one of the events she had recommended we participate in, she introduced me to one of her "friends" who happened to be a TV personality of some sort at the time.

It was a fashion pop up event, held in the parking space of a rather famous supermarket in Lagos.

I was all set up with my clothes on the racks and mannequins all dolled up.

We had music playing and I was generally eye balling any human that walked past my stall, with a Julia Roberts smile plastered across my face, in an attempt to lure them into buying.

Come to think of it, maybe what's why nobody bought, I bet they were secretly thinking, "this beesh look crazy, what kind of crazy smile is this?"

Oh well, their loss.

Anyway, this her friend Sade, walks up to my rack and I immediately went up to her, "hi, how are you? Nice to meet you", I said.

She smiled back and we exchanged all the pleasantries.

Sade had a friend with her, who was already at my cloth racks, looking through the pieces I had on display.

With each one they'd tell me how lovely my "stuff" really is and how talented I am.

I'm just standing there smiling, thinking to myself, "ehn thanks a lot, buy something then".

Lol

Eventually, Sade's friend pulled out a pair of denim trouser she liked, asked for the price and changing room.

It was the perfect size and fit for her and she wanted it.

She came back from the changing room, asked me for a discount off the trouser.

In my mind I went, "what? are you phecking serious?"

But then I said out loud "weeeeellll, okay I guess I can take something off"

Wuss.

Desperado.

That was me.

I gave her the discount, she paid and I packed it up.

I was happy, that was my first sale.

As they were walking towards the exit, Sade spots a cute sleeveless denim vest on the rack and showed it to her friend, who agreed it would go well with the trouser she just bought.

They both turned to me and I knew exactly what was about to come out of their mouths.

She wanted the vest for free.

And I would have said no too, but my PR lady sensed that and interjected, reminding me that Sade has a large following on social media as a result of her job.

It would be in my best interest to build a relationship with her aka give her the damn vest.

So I did.

She got a discount on the trouser and got a free vest too.

I was such an astute businesswoman, wasn't I? Smh.

Anyway, that was that, the event ended, we all went our separate ways.

I continued to run my brand and grow it, she continued to do whatever it was she was doing.

Until about a year later, I was at another pop up event and guess who was there too and as a fashion designer?

"Madam" Sade!

Guess what one of her pieces was? My trouser!

This beesh, had copied my trouser in its entirety.

Save the difference in fabric, it was my design she had as one of her collection pieces.

I was livid, I felt used.

But guess what, I didn't do anything. I couldn't.

First, I didn't have a patent to protect my design in place, second, this is the fashion industry, where when you're a small brand like mine, I'm afraid stuffs like this will happen.

What made it even more painful for me was they way she was selling out on it.

My PR lady was right, she had the following on her social media platforms, the conversation to sale was incredible for her, heartbreaking for me.

My friends will see her product aka my trouser, on social media, send me the link and go, "this is yours, isn't it?"

And I'd have to swallow the bitter pill and try to act nonchalant about it so they don't know how painful it is for me.

I didn't do anything about it, just pretended she never existed and eventually I got over it.

I brought out another collection after that.

In fact I brought out many more.

Each of them was a smash hit.

"Back to back hits, a la Olamide" LOL

I got great reviews and accolades.

And I still sold pieces of the ones she copied. Maybe not as many as she did, but I sold.

I didn't allow the fact that she copied my product and sold more quantities than I did to stop me, in fact it made me want to "show her".

To prove to her that she was nothing more than an untalented, unoriginal copy rat.

And the only way to do that was to double down on my work and do an even better job than I did before.

Never let the fear of people stealing your idea stop you from following your dreams.

Your talent comes from a pool that will never run dry and you'll be doing yourself a disservice by not improving and growing.

In truth, someone copying your work at any level, in any format should translate to you the fact that it was good enough.

Because I'm pretty sure no one has reproduced Kanye West's nude collection yet.

Just saying.

CHAPTER 11

START APPRECIATING THE TIME OF SMALL BEGINNINGS

My cousin was the president of her Club in University College London and was in charge of their students' annual end of year party.

For that particular year, they had a lot of amazing activities planned, one of which would be a fashion show, followed by some spoken words and music.

Naturally, I was to make her dress for the evening. I mean why spend thousands on a Versace gown when your designer cousin can cook up a stunning bespoke piece for ya eh?

I had both our dresses ready well on time and I was merely counting down the days before I'd have to take that bloody 4 hr train ride from Manchester to London.

Just a few days before the event, my cousin called me in a panic, (she never panicked, she was training to be a doctor).

The designer they had scheduled had cancelled on them and she had to find a replacement.

She couldn't think of anyone else until she had an aha moment.

Her cousin, aka me, could do it.

"She's more than capable", she told me she told herself.

"Hahahahahahahahaha", that was the sound of me laughing my head off while on the phone with TJ wondering if she was drunk or was just trying to prank me.

This girl was serious o.

She started with the, "remember when you made this, when you made that" journey down memory lane, in an attempt to convince me of my designing superpowers.

LOL

It was actually adorable.

I waited for her to finish and calmly reminded her that, for one I had only ever made clothes for my family members and close friends, I knew absolutely nothing about putting a collection together, and I definitely didn't think it'd be possible with just a few days left to the event.

She was really desperate and she won't take no for an answer. In fact, as far as she was concerned, it was a done deal.

So I thought, "well, I guess I can put some of these fabrics I have together and make some dresses. How crazy can it be?"

I was scared to death but I was also excited.

And so it began, the next few days were intense.

I was glued to my small electric machine in our dining room making a mess everywhere. You couldn't have a peke peke machine disturbing the piece of the neighbour, you'd probably end up in jail.

I managed to put together 8 dresses that I thought would appeal to the young doctors in training, as well as carry across the underlining tone of resilience and love of life.

With my treasures in a suitcase, I headed to London on the day of the event, went straight to hall to meet with my cousin who was already there waiting.

We had no fitting, we just eyeballed the models and started dressing them up.

To my shock and delight, the clothes were perfect fits on the models. I almost cried.

The fashion show was a hit, in fact it was such a hit that every single piece of that "no name" collection was bought.

I went back home with an empty suitcase.

Sometimes in life, opportunities will come that will challenge your belief in yourself and your capabilities, embrace that fear, and do it anyway.

Yes, yes you've heard that a million times.

And? Hear it again.

Embrace the fear, the doubts, the insecurities and do it anyway.

You will never discover your strength or even your weakness, if you never try.

Don't say I didn't tell you.

Okay, now flip the page.

CHAPTER 12

START DEVELOPING A PROCESS

I sold out those pieces in the impromptu collection I showed at UCL that night, even the dress I made for my cousin generated at least 3 leads that I managed to convert to sales.

As a result, my butt was on fire and I decided I was going to roll out my collection. (This is the fashion lingo for produce multiple quantities of the garments).

I did some research, found a manufacturer, consequently went there to inspect the factory.

I was happy with what I saw.

Next, I made a call to Nigeria to order the fabrics I wanted because I wanted to use some traditional Nigerian fabrics, a few of which I had used for the UCL collection pieces.

Back to the factory.

The factory manager informed me that they couldn't use my patterns that I sent to them, because they weren't "professional enough".

He however, conveniently, had a guy the factory uses, so he could "help me out" by sending my "not so professionally drafted" patterns to that guy.

He will redraft and send back to the factory.

The way I thanked this man eh? You will think he just gave me the entire world.

The thing is, I was a newbie at this whole thing as a result, I believed he was helping me out massively.

Since I wholeheartedly agreed to this arrangement, we proceeded to the next stage of the production process; sampling.

Again, he wouldn't use my samples and insisted that they would make a proper sample of each garment instead, based on my sketches.

After i quality check and approve them, those would be the line production samples.

Hmm.....

Of course I knew I'd have to pay for these samples as well, but "I'll do them for you for a fraction of what I usually charge", he promised me.

Again, I agreed.

Yeah, the newbie disease was serious.

I was going back and forth on that dreadful 4 hour train ride from Manchester to London, calling this man to check progress and get updates.

To add to all these hassle, I had university, plus three other odd jobs I was doing.

After about 3 weeks, the patterns were finally ready, I paid the pattern guy.

Gave the go ahead for sampling to begin, "that would take another 3 weeks, for a 12 piece collection", I was told.

When I sent them the product specifications, I made sure I informed them that I wasn't using standard fashion industry body measurements.

I varied mine a little, after a bit of research, to accommodate curvy (not fat o, calm yourself) women as well as slim ones.

So imagine my horror when this dude sent me the first samples and size 8 was more or less made for a long, lean, no boob, no ass, no shape mannequin woman.

I was pissed.

The samples went straight back in the box they came in.

Phone in hand, a scowl that could scare a whole army on my face, I marched to London to have a word with this man. (Well I didn't march really, but you get the point).

This dude was trying to justify the fact that he took it upon himself to adjust my measure to because they weren't the industry standard, "you should be happy that I regulated them for you", he said to me.

Imagine my astonishment, like mister, did you lose your phone?

You could have called me, before making yourself lord and emperor over my business.

The samples had to be remade, this time at his expense. I got the sizes i asked for for each piece.

6 weeks later, the entire production was done.

I got my garments.

After the whole process had been concluded, I eventually found out that, for almost everything he had done, I was way overcharged.

Like, the guy went to market on my head. He saw a newbie who didn't know better and he took that opportunity with both hands to milk it.

I really should have done my own homework with several options to play against each other, so I guess it served me right eh?

(If you nodded yes to that, close my book and never speak to me again lol).

Still didn't matter too much.

I was already super excited, my feet were not touching the ground.

My very own first official collection as a registered fashion designer.

Wowza!

I immediately organized a photoshoot, thankfully I had the baddest photographer as my sis. I mean this girl has her work already featured in top UK magazines.

We rounded up models, put a team together and shot the look-book.

Then I uploaded them onto my website with prices, descriptions and whatnot.

"Now, let the selling begin", I thought to myself with a smile.

And then.............

Nothing.

Yep, first month, second, third month, nothing was happening.

My gorgeous collection and uber professional website was just sitting there.

No click, no sale, no "hello there what the heck are you selling?"

"What is happening? Why isn't anyone buying my clothes? Are they not good enough? Don't they like me?", this was me driving myself insane with questions and worry.

You know those demoralizing questions and unresourceful states we put ourselves when things go wrong?

Yep. I was there.

Wallowing in self doubt, pity and feeling like the entire world was against me.

A whole year passed, and I still didn't get one sale from that website or that collection.

In fact I had people ordering other pieces from me, as a bespoke service, but somehow this collection just sat there.

Eventually, a friend of mine who had remembered the show was asking questions around about my brand.

She found me, we discussed business well enough I guess, because she referred me to a friend of hers who was opening an independent fashion boutique.

 The friend was happy to stock some of these UCL pieces.

How did it all go so horribly wrong you ask, well, I didn't do my homework.

I didn't do proper research before I jumped in and invested tons of time and money.

I let my emotions overpower my intelligence.

"Since I'm super passionate and uber excited about this collection, people will see it and just rush en mass to my website to buy", I had convinced myself.

WRONG!

What I didn't do was figure out how exactly to go about putting together a collection, creating a process that will take that collection from idea conceptualization, all the way to actual individual sale of each piece.

I didn't even have any process in place., in fact I didn't know I needed to have a process. It was a gigantic miscalculation on my part and I paid for it dearly.

People are not mind readers, and they certainly won't buy your product simply because YOU are passionate about it.

They'll buy because it takes care of a certain issue for them.

And not only that, you need to make them aware of it.

They need to know when, where, and why your product exists.

As with everything, preparation is key.

And not just anyhow preparation, a proper, adequate preparation tailored exactly to the task at hand is imperative.

CHAPTER 13

START PERFECTING RELATIONSHIP MANAGEMENT

Me: "Where am I going to get this money from, I'm sucked dry, frustrated and don't know what to do. I mean, what am I doing wrong?".

I was standing in front of my mirror one morning, after a long bout of bawling when I started asking myself these questions.

Frustrated, exhausted and borderline depressed, it felt like nothing was going right. I needed help and I needed it fast.

"Okay Jadesola, you're not giving up now after working for a whole year at KFC in Deansgate, while studying full time in Uni. Screw that! Now think", that was me to myself.

I was in Tony Robbins mode.

I picked up my phone, started calling up some of the people on my contact list I felt could help me out.

My first call was to "Uncle" Sogo.

He happened to be my sister's good friend, he used to come pay her visits once in a while on his way back from work (it was to come eat some Nigerian food really, but whatever).

I knew him to be a pastor because he would not stop telling us about it.

Why call him "Uncle" you ask? Well, as Nigerians, when it comes to showing respect to people that are older than us, they automatically become "uncle" or "aunty".

Call them by their names and you shall receive the smacking of a lifetime.

So, the phone call....

Me:
Good morning Uncle Sogo
(Not his real name, let's protect his marriage from collapsing shall we? Lol)

Uncle Sogo:
Haaaaa my sister, how are you?
Pele.
God bless you.
How have you been?

Me:

Great, Uncle. How's Aunty and the kids? (bla bla bla).

I need your help Uncle, I have a project on hand and I'm running low on cash to fund it.

A couple of things came up unexpectedly and so I need some help with funds.

Could you help me with xxxxx amount of money as investment, i am happy to give it back with some interest that we can both agree on.

Uncle Sogo:

Ah ah, that's not even a lot of money.

Of course.

We'll discuss that in a bit.

Wow, my dear sister, you are sounding great o.

Are you still going to church?

Me:

(inwardly rolling my eyes, what's church got to do with this now, but still I answered).

Yes I am.

After a bit more small talk (mostly him blabbing on and on)

Uncle Sogo:

Ah, pele.

So do you have a boyfriend?

Me:

(surprised) ummm Uncle......

Uncle Sogo:

Eh hen now.

That boy that was chasing you that time.

You know I have always liked you.

But you wouldn't even talk to me those times i came to your house.

You would just leave as soon as I entered your house.

Ehn? Fine baby....

Me:

(Pukes a little in my mouth, yuck!)

With a disgusted laugh masked as a silly one I replied him.

"No o Uncle Sogo, haba"!

You were there to visit my sister now.

Uncle Sogo:

Eh ya.

So what are you doing now?

This is an early call o.

Me:

I'm actually getting ready to leave for work, I wanted to do this before my day gets busy.

Uncle Sogo:

Eh hen. Pele kú isé. (It means "Well done" in Yoruba language)

Let me call you back in a second.

Almost immediately, he calls back this time as FaceTime video call. (See your fault now, Steve Jobs? Lol).

Uncle Sogo:
Eh hen.
I wanted to see your pretty face.
Ah u are ready for work truly.
You look nice o.

Me:
Thanks, Uncle Sogo

Uncle Sogo:
Sooooo....Show me something nowwww

Me:
(Eyes wide in confusion/shock).
Sorry I don't understand.
What do you mean?

Uncle Sogo:
See ehn, you need someone to take care of you, all these wahala that you're doing with work.
I can take care of all this for you.
I like you.
Shey you understand now.
Ehn?
Beautiful baby.
Let me see breast now ehn?
Show me your beautiful breast.

Me:
What?
Uncle Sogo, what the pheck?

Huh?

Are you serious?

I should show you my breast, because I'm asking for funding for my business.

Are you sure it's only breast you want to see?

kiss my teeth

Wow.

I have to go now.

Thanks.

Then I hung up.

I immediately called up my virtual assistant Siri for some quick tasks.

(She became my assistant the day I paid for my iPhone, yup! Argue with your android phone).

Me: Siri, edit contact

Siri: Which contact would you like to edit

Me: Uncle Sogo

Siri: Okay

Me: Change name Uncle Sogo to Mr. "LetMeSeeBreast"

Siri: Uncle Sogo changed to Mr. "LetMeSeeBreast"

Me: Thank you

Siri: Anytime

Lol (Siri is savage, I tell you).

❖

The moral of my epistle is, don't be desperate.

Even when everything seems to be falling apart, when you approach people for help, do not sell your soul to the devil.

Sometimes, they come in the shape of uncles, pastors, mothers, sisters, mentors, even former bosses or colleagues.

The situation doesn't have to automatically degenerate to "he is dead in my books".

Learn to deal with such people in a manner that doesn't compromise your values.

Know when to walk away and approach the issue from a different perspective.

Most importantly, keep pushing forward and don't ever give up, even when they refuse to give you money because your breasts were no show.

Lol.

CHAPTER 14

START REALIZING ISÉ KÓ L'OWÓ (HARD WORK DOES NOT EQUAL MONEY OR SUCCESS)

I was sitting in front of Solo's machine, waiting for him to finish the work I gave him, so I could proceed to putting the finishing touches on them, before sending off to the client.

The morning had been really grey. In fact, I got to work drenched because it had been raining and I wasn't prepared to wait it out in the car.

Time is more precious than money.

For the second time that morning, the sky opened up and poured relentlessly. I sat and marvelled at the greatness of the universe.

As the rain poured down you could just see in the distance, the sky slowing changing from that dark gloomy grey to a slightly lighter shade.

"Maybe, sometimes when we're in the midst of what we perceive as a dark mood, is it possible that all we need is a bit of time to allow the "rain pour" to change our dark greys to a lighter colour?", I thought.

Anyway, I was in that zen/yoga mode when one of the other guys working alongside Solo said...

"Dis kain rain, person suppose just dey house Dey sleep o"

This in pidgin English translates to, "he should be at home subtler up under the covers in this sort of weather condition".

I looked up at him with a smile and asked, "Really, Sleep? When you're meant to be at work? If you're home sleeping because it's raining outside, how do you plan to support yourself and your family when the need arises?"

He looks at me, scoffs and replied in Yoruba.

"Aunty Jadesola, isé kó l'owó o" translating to, "Work is not equal to money".

He was trying to tell me that being rich or successful is not as a result of hard work.

My initial reaction was "this nigga is drunk" LOL
But then I thought to myself "ehn, madam but wait though. In a way he's right, success does not come from hard work, it comes from smart work".

You could log in 500 gazillion hours in a year doing what you love, if it's not done smartly, you may find you're still oscillating back and forth like a pendulum, without any real progress.

When I started my business, I literally would work 21 hour days minimum, flitting from one task to another, always feeling like I was stuck in one mode.

I hadn't learned how to work smartly.

It's was excruciating because I was always tired and frustrated, until I learned to work smartly.

I still work long ass hours but the difference now is, when I do I see results.

It doesn't feel like I wasted my time and energy, and I definitely don't end up wanting to punch the wall at the end of the day, because I couldn't really put a finger on something that seemed to be working well.

I will say this again, time is not money, that's a load of bull.

Time is more precious than money.

Start to use yours wisely.

CHAPTER 15

START TESTING YOUR BOUNDARIES

2 years after I resigned from my 9 to 5 job to go full throttle on my entrepreneur journey, I was balling.

Business was going great.

Although, I hadn't made my first million in profits yet, I no longer needed to sub the business expenses with my own money.

Money coming in was enough to run the business and keep it going, and the next step was to create a profit making strategy.

I thought to myself, "a little expansion is in order at this point, Madam Jadesola".   And out came the pen, paper, calculator and my thinking cap.

I started compiling a list of what I wanted to achieve, when I wanted to achieve it, and how it was going to happen.

With at least three different scenarios lined up, one after the other, I began to break them down into sub components and the resources that each of those components would require.

I then started the elimination process by doing a pros and cons analysis.

Long story short, so I don't bore you out of your brains with business lingo, I decided to put the "so called expansion", the new office in a city nearby.

That option seemed to have the potential of bringing in the most profit from invested revenues, (more business lingo, yes yes! You will have to deal with it), by reducing cost of Labour drastically.

My mentor agreed that it was a good decision, and together, we carefully went over the details one more time, to smooth out some of the kinks.

"Great thinking, Jadesola, I'm super excited for you", he complimented me.

And the process began.

The office space was paid for, and renovations began in earnest to turn it into a functional space for my business.

Equipments were bought and trucked in, connected and ready for workers.

"Now, I need very skilled workers", I breathed out a tired sigh of relief after a very long day on site.

Thankfully, I had put in motion, the process for recruitment such that by the time the equipments were seated in the new office, all that would be left would be to interview workers and confirm employment of the capable ones.

Lord in heaven, my mind was blown.

Not in a good way.

It's not an exaggeration when I tell you that, every single one of the applicants interviewed barely made a cut off mark of 60%.

What was more astounding, is the fact that they all kept bragging about where they had been trained and how many years of experience they had.

My dad had once told me a story of one of the boys he went to primary school with. He was so bad that the principal had written on the boy's testimonial, "the finished product is not better than the raw material because it seems xxxx passed through school, but school did not pass through him".

Ouch, right?

Well, interviewing these guys for my business, I knew exactly, and felt, probably exactly what that poor principal felt.

After interviewing about 10 applicants, all with results within the same range, it started to dawn on me that I may have to review my recruitment rules and be a bit more flexible.

"Okay, let's reduce the cut off mark but increase on-boarding training period I usually give new employees", I told myself.

I would be training everyone I finally employ anyway, even if their final scores meet my expectation, extending and intensifying for these umm, special recruits seemed a logical option.

It was a risk that would cost me more than I had planned for and stretch my budget, but I reckoned it would be worth it in the long run.

W R O O O O N N N N G G G G G.

I employed 5 of them and put them straight into training.

During that period, we didn't take on clients' jobs, that would have been a disaster.

However, products were being generated from the training, these were still costs incurred on the business.

By the second month I was getting frustrated.

Why?

Not only did I have to run the main office, I was also having to race back and forth between the two offices.

It seemed they couldn't get anything done unless I was there.

Every minuscule decision they we're calling me about.

The manager suddenly needed managing.

I was bleeding out money and I was getting quite frustrated.

Oh boy, let me stop right here to say a big thank you to the Lord, God in heaven. For keeping me away from jail as a result of possibly slapping some people so hard their eyes fall out.

I went back to the drawing board.

"What could I do to try and save this situation, somehow, there has to be another way to make it work", I thought.

I switched the strategies around, put some new ones in place.

I was desperate to pull out the nail that was being hammered down, clearly indicating that I may need to shut down operations in the new office.

We carried on like that for a whole year, managing the situation as best as was possible.

However, there really wasn't much else to do.

I fought hard, explained away my rationale to my mentor and anyone else who dared ask me (yes, dared ask me because I was pissed off about the whole situation).

The people I employed just weren't well equipped.

Frankly? They were not qualified for the job, though I was willing to take a risk, the business was suffering.

The conditions in a fresh job seekers pool wasn't promising either, as we tried to recruit a new batch of workers.

Eventually, it had to be done.

I ordered the office locked, all employees dismissed.

A week later, I was sitting at my desk in the studio, driving myself absolutely insane trying to figure out how I could have gotten it so wrong.

The idea was such a great one, it seemed easy enough to execute.

"What went wrong?", I mused.

It took a while for me to come to the realisation that, it wasn't the right time for an expansion really.

The crucial resource needed to make it work after set up was time, which I didn't have.

For it to have come together, I would have had to be hands on in the training, then set up so that everyone involved knows exactly what's needed and expected of them.

My brand wasn't big enough or ready for an expansion where I could just put other people in charge without me physically being there to supervise.

At least, to the point where I know the standard is acceptable, especially in another city.

I learnt that lesson hard, and I warned myself not to make such mistakes again.

Some time later, during a session with my mentor dissecting this colossal failure (at least that was how I perceived it), he asked me the most insane question.

"Why did you do it? Why did you decide to go for it? Were you absolutely sure it was the right decision?", he asked.

It took me a bit to come up with an answer, because the first set of responses that came to me sounded more like excuses even to myself.

I looked at him, "I don't know, I wasn't sure it would work out, but I had to try right?", I answered him.

"There you go, Jadesola" he said.

"You took a risk, it just so happens that this one didn't pan out the way you envisioned it. Doesn't mean that others will not work out", he concluded.

Running a business in any form is a risk you're taking daily.

You're risking your happiness, your stability, your success and even your name on this venture where you have no guarantee of success.

But life in itself is a risk.

You go to bed at night, risking not waking up in the morning.

But we still do it.

Everyday.

Some more than once in a day (you're one of them people aren't ya? Lol).

But don't ever stop taking risks otherwise you'll stay in one spot for the rest of your life.

Only make sure you take calculated risks.

For this one, I just shook my head and thought to myself, the way I calculated this one that flopped ehn, my calculator broke sef.

But I have heard you, Yoda.

Don't beat yourself up, learn the lessons and apply it next time.

CHAPTER 16

START APPRECIATING THE CONCEPT OF TIMING

There's this one huge problem I always tell myself I have.

"I don't have clothes", I'd cry whenever there's a need to go out.

Not that I don't have enough o, it's just that each time I have an event to attend I'm like, "I don't have anything to wear".

Thankfully with my work that never becomes a problem that requires anyone's credit card.

I simply walk into my studio 2 hours before the event, and cook something up.

A mere mortal will think that's not such a good idea, because it could indicate that I'm not always prepared.

You are a goddess, you're not thinking that.

Right?

Shortly before Christmas a few years ago, wait, I think it was last year, lol.

My mentor informs me that his wife would love it if I could come spend the day with them.

I prefer to have a quiet reflective time to myself over the Xmas and New Years holiday, because my family members are mostly out of the country. A couple of days in consideration of the offer, I finally responded.

"It'd be my pleasure, please extend my thanks to your wife. I'll see you guys on Xmas day", I texted back to him.

As I got engrossed in massive pre-holiday orders, it completely flew off my mind, so guess what happened on Christmas Eve?

I suddenly went "oh my God, I don't have anything to wear".

Made a mad dash to my stock room for fabric, went into the studio and just did my thang.

It was a simple enough dress, long-sleeve, form fitting pencil dress.

That's my vibe, no fuss, chic and super hot outfit.

Yep!

(If you were planning to surprise me with a gift there you go. Lol).

On Christmas morning, I went through my usual routine, only this time I had plenty of time, so no need to rush.

I brought my lovely new dress out with a gorgeous pair of heels.

"Let's do this Jadesola", I was ready to roll.

Suddenly, with an intensity I could liken to being suddenly enveloped by the strongest wave in the ocean, I felt this heaviness surround me.

I flopped down on the edge of my bed and started bawling.

What happened, the dress reminded me of my mum.

Not that I had forgotten her or that I ever could.

Somehow that morning, looking at the dress I made using her fabric, was just a bit too much.

I couldn't go my mentor's place,

"I can't make it, Edward", I cried to him on the phone.

As soon as he heard my broken voice, he told me it was okay, he understood.

I put my dress back in the closet and that was it.

Time passed, I went back to work, life went on.

One day, during a photoshoot for some pieces from my collection, my Xmas dress somehow shows up on the rack.

I was never going to put it on the rack for sale, but I just wanted to shoot it.

Anyway, I went to change into the dress and sauntered out of the changing room, shut the door behind me like I was Naomi Campbell.

My mentor was in my office that day, consulting with my best friend.

He mentors her too.

Yes, we have great taste, my bestie and I.

They were both on their knees looking at some papers they had spread out on the floor.

I guess the sound of the door closing was enough to make them both look up, because they both did, at the same time.

Both of them froze, mouths and eyes wide (mostly mentor's mouth), starring at me.

"Umm What is wrong, did I put my dress on backwards?", I looked down at myself, trying to figure out the cause of their shock.

Nothing was wrong that I could see, still, they were starring at me.

I was so confused.

As though they were both ticking to the same clock they both said "oh my God", at the same bloody time.

Mentor: "Jesus Jadesola, that dress is incredible".

Tola: "I don't have any words". (That beesh always has words okay?).

Now the thing is, I see these guys at least 4 times in a week.

They know my work, they've seen me in countless outfits, of varying shapes and hues.

They have seen me in the most glamorous looks, as well as the most God-awful ones.

(I have never not looked absolutely GLAM. It's my word against yours).

Back to the shocked faces.

I was so embarrassed, that I could swore my melanin rich face was turning a serious shade of pink.

I ran (I actually did) back into the changing room and took the dress off and decided right there and then, it wasn't for public consumption.

Right now if you ask me, I couldn't tell you why.

I just knew from then that it was forever going to be my special dress.

They laughed at me, asked why I reacted that way.

Then they laughed some more, as I told them the story and encouraged me to go shoot it.

Which I did.

Despite that, I haven't been able to wear that dress.

It sits in my closet right now, every time I bring it out to wear, I remember their reactions and I quickly put it back.

The way my brain processed that information was, if people that are more or less like family, react that way to the dress, what would a stranger do.

"I don't want to draw any attention to myself", I excused myself.

I really, really don't like it at all.

Some months later, I brought it out and tried it on again, with shoes and accessories and some swag.

I stood in front of the mirror and thought, "what would Mum say if she were here to see what I did with her fabric?"

She always loved watching me work, she always told me how she enjoyed seeing fabric being changed into different forms.

That was enough motivation for me, so much so that I decided to wear the dress out. Anyone someone commented on it I would tell them it belonged to my mum.

It would be one of the many ways I'd keep her memory with me and honor her amazing taste and love of life.

No matter what happens to you, time will not heal. It will show you the path you need to take and will guide you to the lesson that needs to be learned.

Do not rush it, let time do it's thing.

CHAPTER 17

START LEARNING NOT TO BELITTLE YOUR OWN TALENT

Tuesday afternoon, around 2pm I started to panic.

I had Kizomba class in just 4 hours, out of which I need one whole hour to drive there because traffic will not let me be great.

This leaves me with 3 hours and a heartbeat well above normal rate, because once again, "I don't have anything to wear".

Are you sick of hearing this from me yet?

You know nothing Jon Snow, ask my bestie Tola.

I had fabric, I had my studio and I had my sketchbook, "Khalisee, (yup, that was my new persona before she was turned into a mass murderer) let's go do what we do", I morale-d myself up.

Lights on, patterns out, fabric out, scissors and chalk ready, 20 mins later I was sitting by the machine pressing away and jamming to my work mode playlist, aptly named PowerState.

Just barely two hours later I had a dress ready.

It was simple, cute for a tomboyish lanky ass woman like myself.

I wasn't trying to cause any heart palpitations at dance class.

At least, so I thought to myself.

A quick shower and light makeup later, I was on the move.

One of the joys in my life, is the fact that I don't like the pancake people slap on their faces in the name of makeup, for me light powder, eyeliner and signature red lips will do just fine.

By 6.25 pm, I was already at the venue for class, waiting for the session to start.

The class usually holds at some bar that allowed us to use their place, in hopes that we would help drag in clients every time we have class.

So come Tuesday, there were usually quite a few men sitting around the bar, pretending to only be interested in their drinks meanwhile they're using corner eye to look at the women dancing, tightly held by the men as they shake their "Bundas" aka bum.

As I was about 40 minutes early, I decided to wait in my car till class.

"Why didn't you go inside, maybe use that opportunity to network", you're probably thinking as you're reading this.

Well, I wasn't in the mood to be picked up by these randy Lagos men.

Simples!

"How do you know you'll be picked up?"

Well, I own a full length mirror hunnay,

Lol

It wasn't long before the two instructors, Vincent and Alex, plus a few other students entered.

"Okay, move your ass woman", I ordered myself.

The members only access tag was waiting for me at the door which I happily accepted as I faced the entrance.

I couldn't wait to hear the sensual Kizomba music that would be blaring on the speakers.

Vincent and Alex were upstairs talking to some of the other students, "ooh let me go interrupt his conversation", I mischievously decided.

We smiled at each other and exchanged hugs, as is our normal practice.

You have to hug each person as many times as needed.

Alex pulls me a little to one side and goes "babe I love this dress o, wow"

I humbly (*cough) said thanks with a smile, and told her it's one of my pieces.

The conversation then went something like this.....

Alex: Really? Is it on the rack?
Me: No o, in fact i only just made it this afternoon as I didn't have anything to wear.
Alex: STOP IT GIRL. Whaaaaattt? That's amazing. Well I envy you sha o. This stuff is so easy for you.

I smiled and told her not be silly, that I'd hook her up whenever she's ready.

We walked to the dance floor from there and lessons started.

You see, as soon as she said oh it's so easy for you, my default thought was, "not really o, it's super hard and I put a lot of effort into it".

But then I thought, "wait a sec, yes it is hard work but I'm lucky to have a gift that does comes easy to me".

Why am I being disrespectful to God or the universe or whatever brought us all here, by trying to belittle this huge gift and awesome grace I have.

When your success begins to manifest itself, you will hear statements like "you're so lucky", "well this is so easy for you" etc.

Do not argue or try to belittle your talent or gift, or even your hard work, just to make the other person feel comfortable.

By all means bask in the glow of it.

Be grateful and appreciative and then pay it forward.

Yes, I am lucky.

Yes, it comes easy to me.

For that, I'll always be grateful.

CHAPTER 18

START UNDERSTANDING THAT NOT ALL PARTNERSHIPS ARE WORTH IT

I was sitting down minding my own business at this other job I have, where I get to drive super sports cars for fun, well not technically for fun.

We drive these cars and test them out, check all their specs and compare them to other models for the general public.

For those that are interested in driving such cars, at least.

This particular shoot was going to be so much fun, we had my favourite car brand, Mercedes on hand to drive.

We had the G63 Brabus, you know the one with twin turbo 4.0 litre V8, with a whopping 789 hp running 0 - 100 in 4.1 secs?

You don't?

Do I even want to meet you at all?

LOL

Waiting for set up to finish, it was hot as pheck. Who cared? I was buzzing to get behind the wheels.

One of the other presenters walked up to me, said hello and proceeded to engage me in small talk.

My spirit literally stepped out of my body, stood in front of me and asked, "why the heck are you responding to small talk when you have that gorgeous beast over there to go admire?"

Had to calm madam spirit Jadesola down.

Jesus said strangers deserve some respect, too right?

I found out that Anthony was into business branding and media productions, he was interested in politics and was, at some point, going to run for the position of district counsellor in his area. He was also planning to launch one of his businesses that was in the pipeline.

Yup, big ambitions.

Eventually, he stopped talking to me, in time to reconcile with my true love that was sitting pretty mere yards away, patiently waiting for me to come and drive her.

The shoot was every bit as much fun as I expected. We all said our goodbyes and faded into the hot Lagos sun once more.

About two weeks or so after the shoot, Anthony called me up, he wanted to meet for drinks.

"Hmmmmm, Mr Big shot, what dost thou want?"

We went out a couple of times and I soon realized that, as cool as he appeared, dude was scared shet of commitment.

Me? I had had enough of commitment phobics, I wasn't going to get myself entangled in such a nasty web of unproductive relationships again, so I quickly retraced my high heel clad steps and backed off.

No be fight abi?

After a few more weeks of him trying to drag me back into it with him, I read the riot act to him.

Made it clear to him what I was looking for in a guy, since he didn't seem ready or interested in providing that, there was no need wasting each other's times.

"Bye Adam, this eve has to move on", I told myself.

We left it at that, and remained cordial.

A while later he reached out to me that, he had a business proposition he wanted to meet at some cafe in town to discuss about.

He had a product prototype developed, to sampling stage, but he neither wanted to be the face of it or nor be involved in the operation running of the brand, he wanted me to spearhead it.

I reviewed the product, it looked like a good one but needed redesigning before it could be pushed into production.

He offered me partnership.

He was only interested in being the financial investor and would be happy with me being the face of the brand, as well as running the business.

A 4-hour long meeting got us to the point of deciding on the structure and processes for the business.

We immediately created a To-Do list, which we assigned to ourselves for actions.

Week one, I checked in to see how far he had gone. Nothing had been done, but he promised he was on top of it.

Week two, same response.

"Okay, hold up", I thought.

I had multiple other businesses I was running and this dude isn't about to complicate my life further with this rubbish.

I called an emergency "board meeting".

"Anthony, I can't work this way, you're already not pulling your end of the rope. Are we doing this the right way or not?".

He was busy, and waiting on some other people to come in with some resources, this and that, those were his reasons for slacking.

Fine.

What do we do? We can't keep the plan on hold if we hope to launch fully by the agreed date.

I suggested that he continues to chase those resources and I'd proceed with the redesign.

Like clockwork, I finished the redesign within the assigned time and sent the details to him.

He loved them and we both agreed the product was much better that way, it was more or less a new one.

Now sampling time, dude was still "chasing resources".

To avoid further delays, I offered to fund the sampling process, he would reimburse me from the business pocket once the resources comes in.

We both agreed.

Back and forth this went on, until it started to dawn on me that this dude wasn't going to get anything done.

He couldn't follow through on plans, was quite flaky and was just wasting my precious time.

It didn't take long before he received a message from me, letting him know I was no longer interested, I wanted to be paid for the samples I had produced and move on.

He didn't think that was a great idea, "You're perfect for this Jadesola", he tried to arm-twist me.

But he was messing with the wrong gal.

When that didn't work to his advantage, he hit me with, "Once I pay for the sample, both the product and sample becomes mine".

I quickly put my Tony Stark brains on and let him understand that his original product is his, but my redesign is mine and as such, he can't use it.

He went from zero to hundred so quick that Brabus couldn't catch us. Then accused me of trying to steal his product.

Meh, I knew my onions so he could kick and scream all he liked, "My lawyer shall be in touch with you, mister".

Back and forth we went for a while, before he finally conceded and agreed to let me have my redesign.

I guess my lawyer did a great job.

He's been in contact since that time (at least trying to get me to respond to him) pleading for us to restart the business with promises that he'd be better.

"Uh, thanks but no thanks".

I had enough already.

Not all partnerships are worth going into.

Don't ask me how you'll know.

You will if you pay attention, because in other aspects of their lives, in little things they do, you'll be able to tell if they have issues that will ultimately affect that partnership.

Keep your mind open, eyes wide and gut centered.

CONCLUSION

For a lot of people, when things happen, they either simply give up or allude it to the fact that it's controlled by forces greater than them.

I used to be one of them.

If you still are, don't despair.

You're not wrong mostly, you're simply overlooking the fact that, that power greater than you, has already gifted you the power to make different choices of how you'll interpret and react to those events.

This issue affects us in all aspects of our lives, and if you're crazy enough to choose the entrepreneurial path, oh man.

If you're still sitting in that big chair, with the school of thought that running a business simply means having a really great idea, putting it together and then waiting for it to magically take off after the smallest nudge, to blossom into a full fledged empire, please get up and get out right now.

Situations will frequently come up, where you will be pushed. Pushed hard and flat against the most difficult obstacles, you will want to throw in the towel and give up on your dreams, especially when you're just starting out.

Don't.

If it seems like it's only happening to you, or it keeps happening, it's because the universe has a way of repeating the events if it appears you're not picking up on the lessons quickly enough.

No matter what gets pushed in your path, there are major building blocks upon which the foundation of your success will be laid.

Here they are:

- Your mind needs to be in the right frame, your outlook on events, the way you break them down and how you use them as your reference point.
- What exactly is the solution you're bringing and in what way is it going to make a difference.
- What are the steps involved in moving from one point to the other, what happens if any of those steps get disrupted.
- Each individual you come across will NOT be like you, they most likely will not share your values or perspectives on issues. Does that mean you don't deal with them?
- Life is full of distractions and challenges, can you still waddle through the mud and come out on the other side a winner?

I have many more experiences that I could write God knows how many other books on, but the whole point of this one is to show you that each experience, no matter how crazy, painful, ridiculous, similar or different they are, brings a unique lesson.

I have written this book to sensitize you to all that's happening around you. We have been so beaten down and conditioned by our environments now, that we're all running around on autopilot, and as a result missing out on important happenings around us that will improve the quality of our existence.

Some stories in this book will make you cringe in horror, some will make you laugh and you will mutter to yourself, this woman is insane. But if you look around, you have things happening to you right now that you're not paying attention to, which is probably why you haven't taken that one crucial step towards your greater success.

Listen, the best decision you can make for yourself is to start anyway, despite the fear.

So what are you waiting for now?

Still going to just sit there?

Move your butt!

You gat this.

ABOUT JADESOLA

Do you know Jadesola?

Well technically you do, you know her names and you have seen her pictures, only now you know a little more.

After three gorgeous babies, 2 boys and a girl, her parents still decided they'd not had enough of nappy changes and decided to have another go.

9 months later, this fiery Dragon made her first little roar.

Jadesola Omobolaji Onaolapo
is a successful businesswoman, in varying fields such as coaching and training, fashion, leather crafts and even carpentry.

She is professionally trained as an engineer with multiple degrees and has used all these experiences to push her businesses to a global status.

She is an expert at systems design, entrepreneurial project management, and as a business structure and process development consultant, having previously worked in the oil and gas for more than 12 years before deciding to launch her own business.

She is a masterclass coach and mentor, certified as an epic outcomes matrix result coach and performance consultant for entrepreneurs, especially micro businesses. She currently runs multiple businesses one of which is as the creative director and owner of the international Fashion Label: NIIFFE, a fashion label that started first as a micro enterprise and then grew to become an international business concern.

Omobolaji also co-owns a UK registered charity organisation called HeedAfrica with her sister where they provide free medical checks, consultation and treatment to those who don't have easy and ready access. She's been part of the successful execution of such programs in multiples places in Oyo State, Nigeria as well as Lagos state.

Omobolaji lives between Lagos, Nigeria and New York, USA.

LETS CONNECT

Thank you for buying and reading this book. Please remember to leave reviews and connect with me on my social media platforms:

Mail: jadesola1510@gmail.com
Instagram: @omobolajijadesolaonaolapo
Twitter: @jadebonje
Facebook @omobolajijadesolaonaolapo

Join my Facebook community Micro Business Network™, where I share my knowledge on business, how to start one, launch it and run it successfully, from a micro status to a full fledged global business.

https://www.facebook.com/groups/microbusinessnetwork/

Or if you're just starting out as an entrepreneur, join my online academy Micro Business Academy™, where I take my students from just talking about starting a business to actually launching one in as little as 30 days.

https://www.facebook.com/groups/microbusinessacademy/

www.ingramcontent.com/pod-product-compliance
Lightning Source LLC
Chambersburg PA
CBHW070436180526
45158CB00019B/1466